Lifeline,

Ten Poems by Lesl

Edited by
Mandy Ross and Jo Brookes

Candlestick Press

Published by:
Candlestick Press,
Diversity House, 72 Nottingham Road, Arnold, Nottingham NG5 6LF, UK
www.candlestickpress.co.uk

Design, typesetting, print and production by Diversity Creative
Marketing Solutions Ltd., www.diversity.agency

Selection and introduction © Mandy Ross and Jo Brookes
Cover illustration © Quyen Dinh, www.parlortattooprints.com
Candlestick Press monogram © Barbara Shaw, 2008

© Candlestick Press, 2016

ISBN 978 1 907598 36 4

Acknowledgements:
Our thanks to Mandy Ross and Jo Brookes for suggesting and editing
this pamphlet. Thanks also to Bloodaxe Books for permission to reprint
Josephine Balmer's translation of Sappho, 'Some an army on horseback,
some an army on foot' from *Poems and Fragments* (Bloodaxe Books,
1992). C P Cavafy, 'Comes to Rest', translated by Edmund Keeley and
Philip Sherrard, is from *Collected Poems* (Hogarth Press, 1990) and is
reprinted by permission of The Random House Group Ltd and Rogers,
Coleridge and White. Thom Gunn, 'The Hug', from *The Man with Night
Sweats* (Faber & Faber, 1992) is reprinted by permission of Farrar, Straus
and Giroux. Audre Lorde, 'On a Night of the Full Moon' from *Undersong:
Chosen Poems Old and New* (Virago, 1993) is reprinted by kind permission
of the Abner Stein Agency and W W Norton. Thanks also to W W Norton
for permission to reprint May Sarton, 'The Lady and the Unicorn' from
Collected Poems 1930 – 1993 (W W Norton, 1993). Gregory Woods,
'When You Go' is reprinted by kind permission of the author and Carcanet
Press from *An Ordinary Dog* (Carcanet Press, 2011). John McCullough,
'Masterclass' first appeared in *The Frost Fairs* (Salt, 2011) and is reprinted
here by kind permission of the author. Our thanks to PanMacmillan/
Picador for permission to reprint 'Girl next door' by Kate Tempest, from
Hold Your Own (Picador, 2014) and to Rogers, Coleridge and White for
permission to reprint Carol Ann Duffy, 'White Writing' from *Feminine
Gospels* (Picador, 2002).

While every effort has been made to secure permission to reprint material
protected by copyright, we will be pleased to make good any omissions
brought to our attention in future printings of this pamphlet.

Where poets are no longer living, their dates are given.

Introduction: It happens all the time in heaven

Do lesbian and gay poets always write lesbian and gay poetry? Or only when they write about love? And is same-sex love different from any other love, now that we can get married?

Our ten poets, shown more or less chronologically, give us a glimpse of same-sex loves and lives through history. We can imagine them savouring the poems of those who went before them, as Allen Ginsberg addressed Walt Whitman in 'A Supermarket in California': "dear father, graybeard, lonely old courage-teacher".

Love, fleeting or decades-long, open or clandestine, remembered or anticipated; these poems explore love in many guises. C P Cavafy writes of the passionate "delight of flesh between half-opened clothes"; May Sarton's wistful unicorn lies ghostly with the lady in the tapestry, "most strangely wed", while Gregory Woods hungers wryly for a shared bungalow.

This is a moment to celebrate history's great enlightened shift towards equal marriage. It has been a long and hard-won victory in many western countries, and the struggle is not yet over. In many places around the world, centuries of stigma have not shifted, and same-sex lovers are still cruelly persecuted.

But we shouldn't assume an unbroken history of oppression. In his plea for kindness within marriage, the fourteenth-century Sufi poet Hafiz includes "men and men who are lovers, and women and women who give each other light". He begins, "It happens all the time in heaven…".

Mandy Ross and Jo Brookes

Some an army on horseback, some an army on foot

Some an army on horseback, some an army on foot
and some say a fleet of ships is the loveliest sight
on this dark earth; but I say it is what-
ever you desire:

and it is perfectly possible to make this clear
to all; for Helen, the woman who by far surpassed
all others in her beauty, left her husband –
the best of all men –

behind and sailed far away to Troy; she did not spare
a single thought for her child nor for her dear parents
but [the goddess of love] led her astray
[to desire . . .]

           [. . . which]
reminds me now of Anactoria
although far away,

whose long-desired footstep, whose radiant, sparkling face
I would rather see before me than the chariots
of Lydia or the armour of men
who fight wars on foot . . .

Sappho (615 – 570 BC) translated by Josephine Balmer

from **Song of Myself**

I celebrate myself, and sing myself,
And what I assume you shall assume,
For every atom belonging to me as good belongs to you.

I loafe and invite my soul,
I lean and loafe at my ease observing a spear of summer grass.
My tongue, every atom of my blood, form'd from this soil,
                                                    this air,
Born here of parents born here from parents the same, and their
    parents the same,
I, now thirty-seven years old in perfect health begin,
Hoping to cease not till death…

…Through me many long dumb voices,
Voices of the interminable generations of prisoners and slaves,
Voices of the diseas'd and despairing and of thieves and dwarfs,
Voices of cycles of preparation and accretion,
And of the threads that connect the stars, and of wombs and of
    the father-stuff,
And of the rights of them that others are down upon,
Of the deform'd, trivial, flat, foolish, despised,
Fog in the air, beetles rolling balls of dung.

Through me forbidden voices,
Voices of sexes and lusts, voices veil'd and I remove the veil,
Voices indecent by me clarified and transfigur'd.

Walt Whitman (1819 – 1892)

Comes to Rest

It must have been one o'clock at night
or half past one.
                  A corner in a taverna,
behind the wooden partition:
except for the two of us the place completely empty.
A lamp barely gave it light.
The waiter was sleeping by the door.

No one could see us.
But anyway, we were already so worked up
we'd become incapable of caution.

Our clothes half opened – we weren't wearing much:
it was a beautiful hot July.

Delight of flesh between
half-opened clothes;
quick baring of flesh – a vision
that has crossed twenty-six years
and now comes to rest in this poetry.

C P Cavafy (1863 – 1933)
translated by Edmund Keeley and Philip Sherrard

The Lady and the Unicorn

The Cluny Tapestries

I am the unicorn and bow my head
You are the lady woven into history
And here forever we are bound in mystery
Our wine, Imagination, and our bread,
And I the unicorn who bows his head.

You are all interwoven in my history
And you and I have been most strangely wed
I am the unicorn and bow my head
And lay my wildness down upon your knee
You are the lady woven into history.

And here forever we are sweetly wed
With flowers and rabbits in the tapestry
You are the lady woven into history
Imagination is our bridal bed:
We lie ghostly upon it, no word said.

Among the flowers of the tapestry
I am the unicorn and by your bed
Come gently, gently to bow down my head,
Lay at your side this love, this mystery,
And call you lady of my tapestry.

I am the unicorn and bow my head
To one so sweetly lost, so strangely wed:

You sit forever under a small formal tree
Where I forever search your eyes to be

Rewarded with this shining tragedy
And know your beauty was not cast for me,

Know we are woven all in mystery,
The wound imagined where no one has bled,

My wild love chastened to this history
Where I before your eyes, bow down my head.

May Sarton (1912 - 1995)

On a Night of the Full Moon

i

Out of my flesh that hungers
and my mouth that knows
comes the shape I am seeking
for reason.
The curve of your waiting body
fits my waiting hand
your breasts warm as sunlight
your lips quick as young birds
between your thighs the sweet
sharp taste of limes.

Thus I hold you
frank in my heart's eye
in my skin's knowing
as my fingers conceive your flesh
I feel your stomach
moving against me.

Before the moon wanes again
we shall come together.

ii

And I would be the moon
spoken over your beckoning flesh
breaking against reservations
beaching thought
my hands at your high tide
over and under inside you
and the passing of hungers
attended, forgotten.

    Darkly risen
    the moon speaks
    my eyes
    judging your roundness
    delightful.

Audre Lorde (1934 - 1992)

When You Go

Before the bar staff start collecting glasses
And calling time, as other men prepare
The night's diversion, making random passes,
Approach me with a smile, as if you know
No fear, ask me to share your taxi fare,
      And take me with you when you go.

If we should sit up, practically till dawn,
Discussing literature and world affairs,
Until the final phrase becomes a yawn
And tiredness staunches conversation's flow;
Embrace me, make your weary way upstairs,
      But take me with you when you go.

Before the night is over, having swapped
Positions, taking pleasure to extremes
Until completely beat, and having stopped
Performing, to and fro, our quid pro quo;
Make sure, as you withdraw into your dreams,
      You take me with you when you go.

Although we've tempered the initial thrill,
The future beckons and, against the odds,
It looks as if the two of us are still
Together, hungry for a bungalow.
So when you put your plans in place, for God's
      Sake take me with you when you go.

And even when our hopes run out of time,
And death is just a breath away, the bells
Already muffled and the pit of lime
Already dug, prepare a cheerio —
But count yours truly out of your farewells.
        Please take me with you when you go.

Envoi
        Call me a moron, claim I smell,
        Or tell me my ideas repel.
        I don't mind if you kick or clout me.
        But if at any time you doubt me,
                Go to Hell —
                And go without me.

Gregory Woods

The Hug

It was your birthday, we had drunk and dined
   Half of the night with our old friend
     Who'd showed us in the end
   To a bed I reached in one drunk stride.
     Already I lay snug,
  And drowsy with the wine dozed on one side.

I dozed, I slept. My sleep broke on a hug,
     Suddenly, from behind,
In which the full lengths of our bodies pressed:
     Your instep to my heel,
  My shoulder-blades against your chest.
  It was not sex, but I could feel
  The whole strength of your body set,
    Or braced, to mine,
   And locking me to you
  As if we were still twenty-two
  When our grand passion had not yet
   Become familial.
  My quick sleep had deleted all
  Of intervening time and place.
   I only knew
The stay of your secure firm dry embrace.

Thom Gunn (1929 – 2004)

Masterclass

He never tired of explaining from his stool
the route to an immaculate Guinness.

Tilt your glass at forty-five degrees
to kill the splash. Hold it close

to the spout, avoiding contact. Take the brew
three-quarters up, then leave to settle.

What's done next is the barman's choice.
I liked to guess who he'd escort to the gents –

the young drag queen? The bear?
Toot like chalk on the black lid,

his eyes impish as he crept back to his squeeze
for hugs or squabbles. I'd get yanked in

to arbitrate, to remember whens and hows
while I tipped piled fag butts into bins.

The last time he left abruptly, before I could try
my fancy Shamrock, the stale heat relieved

by a blast of salty air. He never worked out
who he caught the virus from

and he didn't end his final class
with the ideal ratio of white to black.

Twelve years on, I haven't stopped waiting
to finish pouring that pint.

John McCullough

Girl next door

I was seven,
my neighbour was eight.
She stuffed a pair of socks down my pants
and straddled me and called me big boy.

I didn't have a clue what it meant
but I've been dizzy on that feeling ever since.

Kate Tempest

White Writing

No vows written to wed you,
I write them white,
my lips on yours,
light in the soft hours of our married years.

No prayers written to bless you,
I write them white,
your soul a flame,
bright in the window of your maiden name.

'No laws written to guard you,
I write them white,
your hand in mine,
palm against palm, lifeline, heartline.

No rules written to guide you,
I write them white,
words on the wind,
traced with a stick where we walk on the sand.

No news written to tell you,
I write it white,
foam on a wave
as we lift up our skirts in the sea, wade,

see last gold sun behind clouds,
inked water in moonlight.
No poems written to praise you,
I write them white.

Carol Ann Duffy